T0052887

If you were a

Pronoun

by Nancy Loewen
illustrated by Sara Gray

PICTURE WINDOW BOOKS
Minneapolis, Minnesota

pronoun (prōn) a word that takes the place of a noun

Editor: Christianne Jones
Designer: Tracy Kaehler
Page Production: Lori Bye
Creative Director: Keith Griffin
Editorial Director: Carol Jones
The illustrations in this book were created with acrylics.

Picture Window Books
1710 Roe Crest Drive
North Mankato, MN 56003
www.capstonepub.com

Copyright © 2007 by Picture Window Books, a Capstone imprint. All rights reserved. No part of this book may be reproduced without written permission from the publisher. The publisher takes no responsibility for the use of any of the materials or methods described in this book, nor for the products thereof.

Library of Congress Cataloging-in-Publication Data
Loewen, Nancy, 1964-
If you were a pronoun / by Nancy Loewen; illustrated by Sara Gray.
p. cm. — (Word fun)
Includes bibliographical references.
ISBN 978-1-4048-2637-3 (library binding)
ISBN 978-1-4048-2639-7 (paperback)
1. English language—Pronoun—Juvenile literature. I. Gray, Sara, ill. II. Title. III. Series.
PE1261.L56 2006
428.2—dc22 2006003396

Printed in the United States 5979

Looking for pronouns?

Watch for the big, colorful words in the example sentences.

Special thanks to our advisers for their expertise:

Rosemary G. Palmer, Ph.D.
Department of Literacy
College of Education
Boise State University

Susan Kesselring, M.A.
Literacy Educator
Rosemount–Apple Valley–Eagan
(Minnesota) School District

If you were
a pronoun ...

... YOU could throw a party.
YOU would invite
HIM and HER
and THEM and US.
YOU would invite EVERYBODY!

"Come ONE, come ALL,"
YOU would say.
"WE will have a
terrific time!"

If you were a pronoun, you would replace nouns and take the repetition out of sentences.

Without Pronouns

Jessie put Jessie's backpack in Jessie's locker. Then Jessie went to talk to Jessie's friends.

With Pronouns

Jessie put **HER** backpack in **HER** locker. Then **SHE** went to talk to **HER** friends.

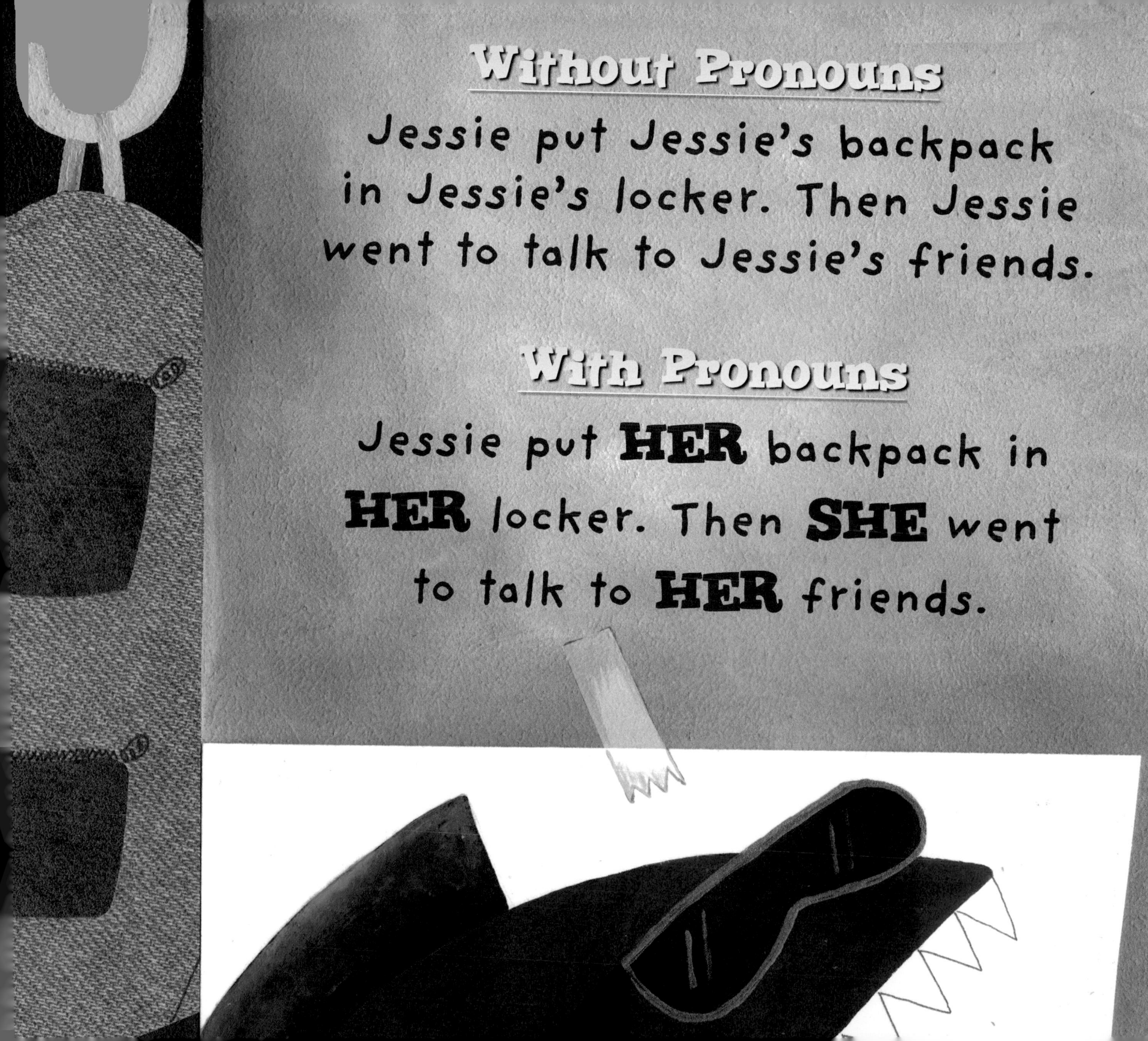

If you were a pronoun, you could take the place of more than one person or thing.

Frank and Dylan each ate
three slices of pizza.

THEY each ate
three slices of pizza.

If you were a pronoun, you could take the place of a person or a person's name. You would be a personal pronoun.

Mrs. Jones handed out the tests.

SHE handed out the tests.

Brian was nervous for the test.
HE was nervous for the test.

If you were a pronoun, you could be possessive. You would let people know that something belongs to someone or something.

Sharky lost some of **HIS** teeth.

OUR playground equipment
needs to be cleaned.

If you were a pronoun, you could tell about people and things without being specific. You would be an indefinite pronoun.

Other common indefinite pronouns include SOMEONE, ALL, ANYONE, NO ONE, ANY, EVERYBODY, NONE, SEVERAL, SOME, BOTH, NEITHER, NOBODY, NOTHING, and MANY.

If you were a pronoun, you could ask questions.
You would be an interrogative pronoun.
WHAT is in here?
WHO understands this stuff?

WHICH is the right one?
WHOM and WHOSE are other interrogative pronouns.

If you were a pronoun, you could point something out without naming it. You would be a demonstrative pronoun.
Please give me THOSE.
I'll take THESE.

THIS isn't it.

If you were a pronoun, you could be like a mirror. You could reflect the subject of the sentence back to itself. The subject tells whom or what the sentence is about.

I can fix it **MYSELF**.

THEY will get **THEMSELVES** into a lot of trouble if THEY eat THEIR textbooks!

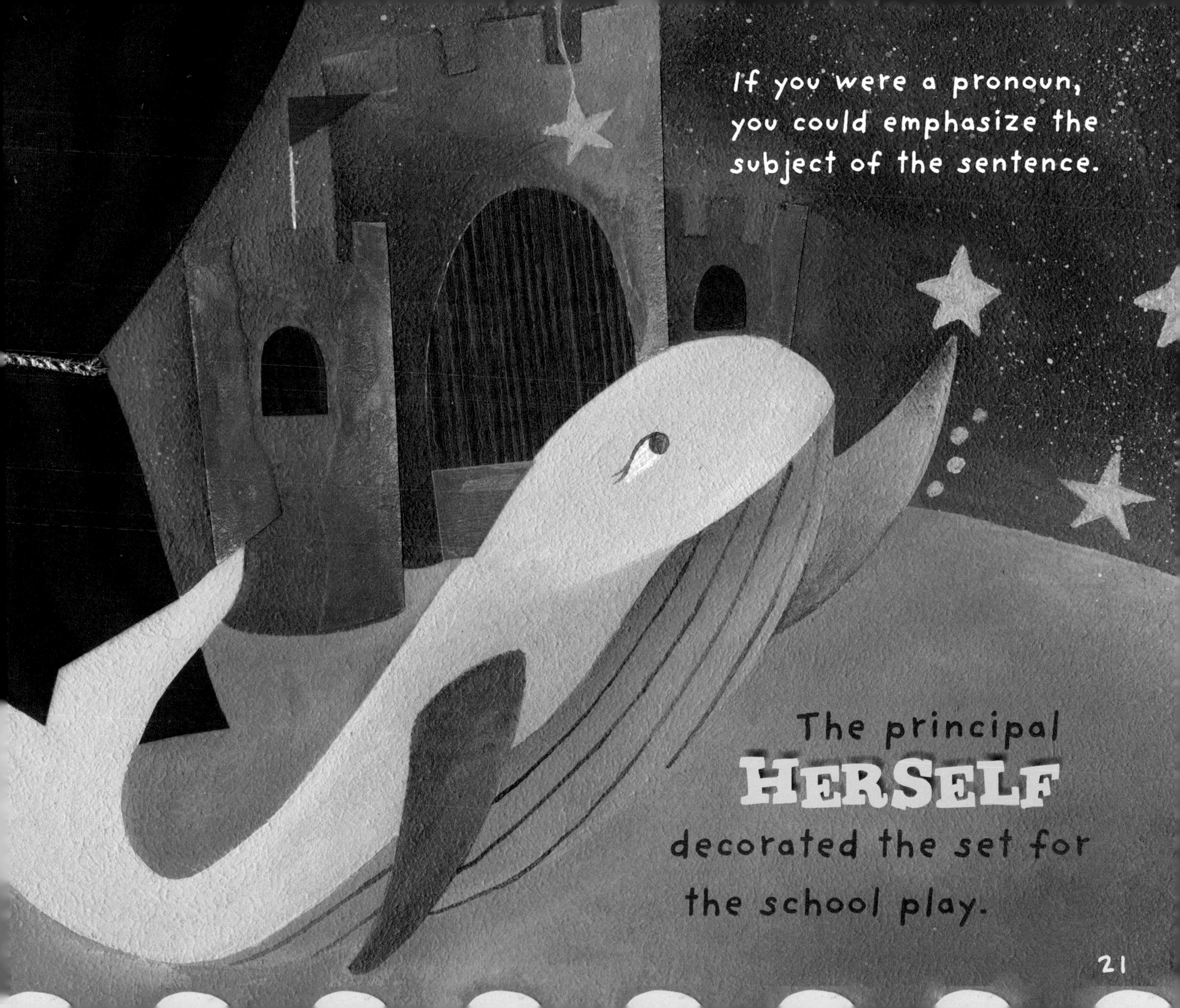

If you were a pronoun, you could emphasize the subject of the sentence.

The principal **HERSELF** decorated the set for the school play.

You would always
be working hard
as a stand-in ...
... if you were

Fun with Pronouns

Gather some friends and some old newspaper or magazine articles.

Give each player a highlighter or a bright crayon.

When someone says go, quickly read through your articles, marking every pronoun you see.

Try doing this for one minute. After one minute, the player with the most pronouns wins.

Fact: If you look up a pronoun in the dictionary, you will see the abbreviation "pron" next to it. The "pron" stands for pronoun.

Glossary

demonstrative pronoun—a type of pronoun that helps point something out without naming it
emphasize—to give more importance to something
indefinite pronoun—a type of pronoun that tells about people and things without being specific
interrogative pronoun—a type of pronoun that asks a question
nouns—words that name a person, place, or thing
personal pronoun—a type of pronoun that takes the place of a person
possessive pronoun—a type of pronoun that shows that an object belongs to someone or something
reflect—to throw back
repetition—to repeat
subject—a word or group of words in a sentence that tells whom or what the sentence is about

Index

pronouns
- demonstrative, 18-19
- eliminating repetition, 6-7
- indefinite, 14-15
- interrogative, 16-17
- personal, 10-11
- possessive, 12-13

To Learn More

More Books to Read

Cleary, Brian P. *I and You and Don't Forget Who: What Is a Pronoun?* Minneapolis: Carolrhoda Books, 2004.

Heinrichs, Ann. *Pronouns.* Chanhassen, Minn.: Child's World, 2004.

Heller, Ruth. *Mine, All Mine: A Book About Pronouns.* New York: Puffin Books, 1999.

On the Web

FactHound offers a safe, fun way to find Web sites related to topics in this book. All of the sites on FactHound have been researched by our staff.

1. Visit *www.facthound.com*
2. Type in this special code: 1404826378
3. Click on the FETCH IT button.

Your trusty FactHound will fetch the best sites for you!

Look for all of the books in the Word Fun series:

If You Were a Conjunction
If You Were a Noun
If You Were a Preposition
If You Were a Pronoun
If You Were a Verb
If You Were an Adjective
If You Were an Adverb
If You Were an Interjection